# Velvet Ant

by Anastasiya Vasilyeva

Consultant: Darin Collins, DVM
Director, Animal Health Programs
Woodland Park Zoo
Seattle, Washington

BEARPORT PUBLISHING

New York, New York

## Credits

Cover, © George Grail/Alamy; 3, © Melinda Fawver/Shutterstock; 4–5, © Herman Wong HM/Shutterstock; 6 (T to B), © Steve Heap/Shutterstock, © Piotr Naskrecki/Minden, © IrinaK/Shutterstock, and © Ger Bosma Photos/Shutterstock; 7, © Edward Snow/iStock; 8T, © magicoven/Shutterstock; 8B, © ANTONIO TRUZZI/Shutterstock; 8–9, © John Abbott/Minden; 10T, © Nature Collection/Alamy; 10B, © Steve Byland/Dreamstime; 11, © James H. Robinson/Science Source; 12–13, © Michel Rauch/BIOSPHOTO/Alamy; 14T, © Sanimfocus/Shutterstock; 14B, © MYN/JP Lawrence/Minden; 15, © Denis Crawford/Alamy; 16, © Adrov Andriy/Shutterstock; 16–17, © Chien Lee/Minden; 18–19, © Piotr Naskrecki/Minden; 19R, © SweetCrisis/Shutterstock; 20, © StGrafix/Shutterstock; 21, © Nature Collection/Alamy; 22 (T to B), © Aldemar A. Acevedo, © Michael and Patricia Fogden/Minden, © oriori/Shutterstock, and © Prillfoto/Dreamstime; 23TL, © Bill Kennedy/Shutterstock; 23TR, © defun/iStock; 23BL, © yevgeniy/Shutterstock; 23BR, © Craig Taylor/Shutterstock; 24, © Melinda Fawver/Shutterstock.

Publisher: Kenn Goin
Senior Editor: Joyce Tavolacci
Creative Director: Spencer Brinker
Design: Debrah Kaiser
Photo Researcher: Thomas Persano

*Library of Congress Cataloging-in-Publication Data*

Names: Vasilyeva, Anastasiya, author.
Title: Velvet ant / by Anastasiya Vasilyeva ; consultant: Darin Collins, DVM, director, Animal Health Programs Woodland Park Zoo Seattle, Washington.
Description: New York, New York : Bearport Publishing Company, Inc., [2018] | Series: Even weirder and cuter | Includes bibliographical references and index.
Identifiers: LCCN 2017034365 (print) | LCCN 2017043472 (ebook) | ISBN 9781684025190 (ebook) | ISBN 9781684024612 (library)
Subjects: LCSH: Mutillidae—Juvenile literature. | Wasps—Juvenile literature.
Classification: LCC QL568.M8 (ebook) | LCC QL568.M8 V37 2018 (print) | DDC 595.798—dc23
LC record available at https://lccn.loc.gov/2017034365

For more information, write to Bearport Publishing Company, Inc., 45 West 21st Street, Suite 3B, New York, New York 10010. Printed in the United States of America.

10 9 8 7 6 5 4 3 2 1

# Contents

What's this weird but cute animal?

It's a velvet ant.

4

Fuzzy body!

Colorful hair!

5

These tiny **insects** only look like big, hairy ants.

They're actually wasps!

common wasp

Velvet ants are covered with fuzz. It can be long or short and vary in color.

7

How big is a velvet ant?

The largest kind is about as long as a paper clip.

The smallest is about the size of a grain of rice!

There are more than 3,000 kinds of velvet ants. They live all over the world.

9

Stay away!

Female velvet ants have giant **stingers**.

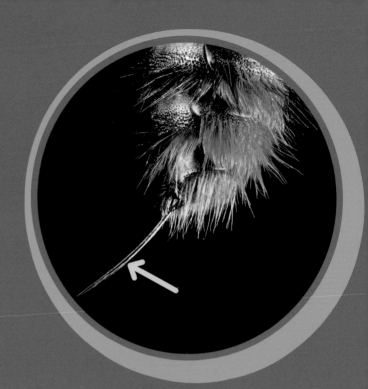

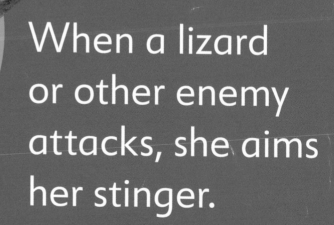

When a lizard or other enemy attacks, she aims her stinger.

Males don't have stingers, but they pretend to sting!

They have a body part that looks and feels like a stinger.

*Ow!*

male
velvet ant

Unlike females, male
velvet ants have
wings. They can fly
away from danger.

13

These hairy wasps stay safe in another way.

They squeak!

The sound scares away attackers.

abdomen

To squeak, the wasp rubs parts of its **abdomen** together.

Velvet ants can also release bad smells to keep enemies away.

15

Under the wasp's fuzz is a suit of armor, or exoskeleton.

It's so strong that most animals can't crush it!

An exoskeleton is the hard outer covering of an insect's body.

16

**exoskeleton**

Velvet ants are powerful, too!

They have strong legs.

When attacked by fire ants, for example, the wasps kick them off.

fire ants

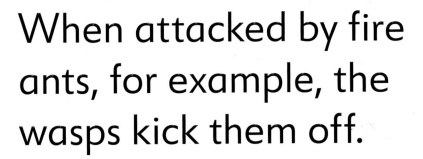

Velvet ants can also escape from enemies by running fast.

19

Sneaky wasps!

Female velvet ants lay their eggs in the nests of other wasps or bees.

After hatching, the velvet ant **larva** eats its host!

*Munch, munch, munch.*

ground bee

If you find a velvet ant, be careful! A bee or wasp nest might be nearby.

21

# More Weird Wasps

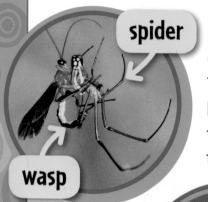

spider

wasp

### Costa Rican Parasitoid Wasp
This Costa Rican wasp can control a spider's brain! The wasp larva injects a chemical into the spider to make it do what it wants. Then the wasp kills the spider and eats it!

### Fig Wasp
These weird wasps are born inside figs. Some chew their way out of the fruit. Then they begin their adult lives.

### Paper Wasp
Paper wasps make their nests from a special kind of paper. They chew up bits of bark and mix it with their saliva. Then they spit out the pulp to build their nests!

# Glossary

**abdomen** (AB-duh-muhn)  the back part of an insect's body

**insects** (IN-sekts)  small animals that have six legs, three main body parts, and a hard covering

**larva** (LAHR-vuh) a young insect that has a wormlike body

**stingers** (STING-urz) the sharp parts animals use for stinging

# Index

# Read More

**Hall, Margaret.** *Wasps (Bugs, Bugs, Bugs!).* North Mankato, MN: Capstone (2006).

**Rustad, Martha E. H.** *Wasps (World of Insects).* Hopkins, MN: Bellwether (2007).

# Learn More Online

To learn more about velvet ants, visit
**www.bearportpublishing.com/EvenWeirderAndCuter**

# About the Author

Anastasiya Vasilyeva is a writer and student who lives near Central Park in New York City. As a kid, she caught ants to keep as pets— but never a velvet ant, of course!